ROMAN LEGION

DAVID ZIENKIEWICZ

National Museums & Galleries of Wales
in association with
The Ermine Street Guard

Amgueddfeydd ac Orielau Cenedlaethol Cymru
National Museums & Galleries of Wales
1995

First published in 1994. Reprinted 1995.
© National Museum of Wales and the individual photographers.

Production: Hywel G. Rees
Design: C.A.P. Daly
Type: New Baskerville
Paper: Consort Royal Brilliance, 150gsm
Printing: McLays and Co Ltd.
ISBN 0 7200 0401 2

The Ermine Street Guard

If you want to find out more about the Guard's activities and performances, contact:

The Ermine Street Guard,
Oakland Farm,
Dog Lane,
Witcombe,
Gloucester GL3 4UG

or telephone either:

The Roman Legionary Museum, Caerleon (01633-423134), or:

English Heritage Special Events Unit (0171- 9733396)

Some further reading

L. Allason-Jones *Women in Roman Britain* (British Museum Publications, 1989)
M.C. Bishop and J.C.N. Coulston *Roman Military Equipment* (Batsford, 1993)
P. Connolly *The Roman Army* (Simon and Schuster Young Books, 1989)
P. Connolly *The Legionary* (Oxford University Press, 1988)
P. Connolly *The Cavalryman* (Oxford University Press, 1988)
R. Davies *Service in the Roman Army* (Edinburgh University Press, 1989)
L. Keppie *The Making of the Roman Army* (Batsford, 1984)
G.R. Watson *The Roman Soldier* (Thames and Hudson, 1969)
G. Webster *The Roman Imperial Army* (A&C Black, 1985)

Front cover: The *centurion* leads the charge.
Rear cover: A *vexillarius* (flag-bearer) of the Second Augustan Legion (LEG II AVG).
Title page: A winged Victory carrying a trophy of captured arms and armour. This bronze plaque was found in the excavation of a centurion's quarters at Caerleon (lent by Mr L. Hill).

Acknowledgements

This book is produced in association with *The Ermine Street Guard,* an amateur group committed to recreating accurately the appearance and drill of the Roman imperial army of the late first century A.D. Many of the photographs were taken at the Roman Amphitheatre at Caerleon, in July 1992, by Tony Hadland (National Museum of Wales, Photographic Department). I am indebted to the English Heritage Special Events Unit for use of photographs taken (by Mike Brown) at Maiden Castle, Dorset in the summer of 1993. These include photographs of the historical re-enactment groups *Brigantia* and *Prytani* (as 'Iron Age Celts'), and *The Troop,* who now provide cavalrymen to *The Ermine Street Guard:* all appear here by kind permission. The text is based in part, and with permission, on a draft written by *Guard* member Clive Constable; and Michael Grant's translation (on p.29) from Tacitus's *Annals of Imperial Rome* (Penguin, 1956), is also reproduced with permission. Chris Haines ('centurion' of the *Guard*) has helped me at all stages of production, and the work benefits much from his enthusiasm.

With the following exceptions, photographs were taken by staff of the Photographic Department of the National Museum of Wales:
Cadw: Welsh Historic Monuments: p.32.1, p.33.3;
Colchester and Essex Museum: p.34.1;
English Heritage Special Events Unit (Mike Brown): p.3.1, p.4.1, p.17.4, p.26.1, p.28.1 and 2, p.29.4;
Ermine Street Guard: p.4.2, p.14.1 and 3;
Gloucester City Museum and Art Gallery: p.34.3;
Paul Karremans: p.18.1, p.28.3;
Mike Knowles: p.36.2;
Gerallt Nash: p.30.2;
National Museum of Wales (David Zienkiewicz): p.6.1, p.9.4, p.14.2, p.16.3, p.26.2, p.33.2, p.36.1;
Barry Wilson: p.19.4, p.20.2;
Geoff Wills: p.27.3, p.30.1 and 3; p.31.4;
David Zienkiewicz: p.35.4.
My thanks to all those who have given permission for their photographs to appear.

This book is dedicated to the men (and women) of *The Ermine Street Guard,* without whose efforts our picture of the Roman imperial army would be dim indeed.

CELTS AND ROMANS

To the Romans, the Celtic inhabitants of Britain were barbarians who could do nothing but benefit from a peace imposed by Roman rule.

The Celts had no written history. They are known to us only from the evidence of archaeology and from the writings of Romans who had as little conception of their ways as, centuries later, did the European invader of the American Indians. The Roman invasion of Britain, ordered by the Emperor Claudius in A.D.43, threatened the extinction of the Celtic way of life. Some tribes quickly conceded to a vastly superior power, and made treaties with the Romans; others held out fiercely for their independence. Hostility to Rome was fuelled by the religious élite, the Druids. Most tribes were eventually conquered, but there was never a time when the whole of the island was subject to Rome.

Celtic tribes were led by hereditary kings and warlords, supported by a warrior aristocracy to whom the mass of the peasantry was enslaved. Warfare was ever-present - with tribal boundaries and alliances changing constantly. There were no standing armies, and warriors were driven mostly by prospect of individual glory. Confrontations tended to be brief, and personal adornment was lavish - ornate helmets and extravagant *torques* (neck-rings). Body armour was rarely worn. To appear more ferocious, warriors painted their bodies and washed their hair with lime [1]. Their weapons were the spear, shield and long slashing sword. Chariots were sometimes used.

Rome maintained the largest professional army of the ancient world. Its men were well-equipped and highly trained, and operated in strict formation on the battlefield [2]. In set-piece battles, Celtic warriors were rarely any match for the Roman army; but in difficult terrain, the Celts excelled in the tactics of guerilla warfare.

This book illustrates the Roman imperial army as it would have appeared in the quarter century which separated the invasion and the foundation of the great legionary fortress at Caerleon - Roman *Isca* - in A.D.74 or 75. It was men such as these who for twenty years campaigned against the two fiercest tribes of Wales - the *Silures* and the *Ordovices*.

4

ROMAN LEGION

The legions of the Roman empire were recruited only from those who had Roman citizenship - but not only from Rome itself. By the first century A.D., many inhabitants of Italy, Spain and Gaul were citizens, too, and were eligible to serve. There were about thirty legions in the Roman army. These were mostly based around the perimeter of the empire, each at its own, neatly laid-out fortress. The British invasion force of A.D.43 comprised four legions accompanied by non-citizen auxiliaries - perhaps 40-50,000 men in all.

The legions were the crack troops of the Roman army - the heavy infantry [1], sent out for campaigns of conquest beyond the empire, or to suppress revolt within its frontiers. A legion was effectively self-supporting. Within its ranks were specialists and craftsmen of all kinds, capable of bringing the mechanisms of Roman rule to a newly-conquered territory - and particularly the engineers and architects who could create the physical infrastructure of a new province.

The basic unit of the legion was the 'section', or *contubernium,* of eight men who shared a room at barracks and a tent on campaign. Ten sections made up a century of 80 men - the essential fighting-unit - which was commanded by a centurion [3]. Ten cohorts made up the legion. Of these, cohorts II to X comprised six centuries (or 480 men), and one - the First Cohort, the most prestigious - comprised five double centuries (800 men). A troop of 120 horsemen, who served as scouts and despatch riders, raised the 'paper strength' of the legion to 5,240. Cohorts on detached duty followed a banner (the *vexillum*) carrying the name of their legion and its 'badge' - for *legio II Augusta* (abbreviated as *LEG II AVG*) this was the capricorn [4].

Legio II Augusta ('Augustus's Own') was founded by the Emperor Augustus - or reformed by him from the remnants of an existing unit, also numbered *II.* With the invasion, *II Augusta* was commanded by Flavius Vespasianus, who won acclaim for his action against tribes in the south-west of Britain. By the time that legion made its permanent base at Caerleon-*Isca* - and after the bloody civil war which followed the death of Nero - Vespasian himself had become emperor. One of the standards carried by the legion bore his image for veneration by the troops [2].

LEGIONARY SOLDIER

A career in the army provided a young man with an ordered and secure future in an uncertain world [1,2,3,4]. Enlistment was voluntary, but the selection process was rigorous. Recruits, normally aged between 18 and 20, had to be fit and of good build, with good eyesight and hearing. A man's chances of selection were much improved if he had a written testimonial from an influential friend or relative.

On selection, a recruit took the 'king's shilling' (*viaticum*) of three gold pieces, and was given a posting to the legion in which he would serve for the next 25 years. On arrival in camp, he and his fellow recruits took an oath of loyalty to the emperor, and began their basic training. At barracks he would share a dormitory, barely four metres square, with the seven men who were to be his comrades-in-arms. The recruit was responsible for providing his own armour and weapons, to minimum standards.

Warfare was intermittent and much of a legionary's service was spent in conditions of peace. Regular training kept every soldier ready for action, and a multitude of chores at camp provided useful work for idle hands. Of his basic pay of 300 silver pieces (*denarii*) a year, most was held back to pay for the soldier's upkeep and equipment, and as compulsory savings to prevent extravagant and immediate spending. But if his spending power was not great, conditions of army life were an improvement on those of his civilian counterpart. The soldier's health and well-being were ensured by a regular and varied diet and by the provision of a hospital, baths and other amenities at camp.

On retirement, at about age 45, many soldiers chose to settle close to the fortress where they had served - and where many had established family ties. Veterans received a cash hand-out of about ten years' pay, or its equivalent in land at a military settlement. With this and their savings, they had to secure their own future livelihood in agriculture or trade. On his death, the legionary was cremated and buried in a military cemetery. Even in death he was provided for, by the burial fund to which he had subscribed during his years of service.

ARMOUR

Even within a single unit, the soldiers' armour was not all the same. Old-fashioned armour was worn by some, and soldiers were permitted to embellish their kit as best they could afford and within approved limits. Many legionaries would have worn the remarkably flexible segmental armour, the *lorica segmentata* [1,3,4]; but others may have worn protective shirts of mail or of scale-armour.

For normal duties in peaceful conditions, the legionary wore a simple short-sleeved, knee-length tunic of wool over a linen undershirt. His open-work boots (*caligae*) were cut from a single piece of leather and laced high up the shin; their thick soles were studded with hobnails. As a concession to colder climates, trousers, socks, and a warm woollen cloak were sometimes worn.

The helmet (*galea*) was made of iron or brass [2]. Hinged cheek-pieces laced together under the chin protected the face, and a reinforcement across the brow served to deflect downward sword-blows away from the nose. A large, close-fitting guard protected the neck. Detachable horsehair plumes were worn mainly for parade.

The suit of body-armour was made up of overlapping segments of thin iron sheet, linked internally by leather straps, and with hinged shoulder plates. All were arranged so as to deflect downward and stabbing sword-blows. With the assistance of a comrade, the *lorica* could be put on over the tunic as a complete unit, and laced together tightly at front and back. It weighed about 10kg, but hardly restricted movement at all. Soldiers would wear the *lorica* even for building duties in hostile areas. When removed, it folded down like a concertina for compact storage.

Arms and legs were left bare, for greater mobility. These were protected mainly by a large and heavy rectangular shield (*scutum*), curved to fit the body. The shield was made of a number of thin sheets of wood, glued together rather like plywood, all encased in leather or linen, and reinforced with metal bindings. A single handle was protected by an iron boss. The shield gave the soldier his primary defence against enemy javelins and arrows, and could be used to push the enemy off-balance and to parry sword-blows. It was used, with others, in interlocking, defensive formations such as the *testudo* (or tortoise).

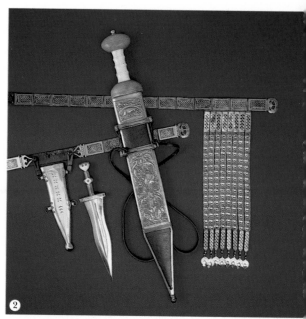

WEAPONS

The legionary's personal weapons - two javelins, a sword and dagger - were designed for use in the battle-line primarily, rather than for individual combat. As the massed ranks of the legion closed on the enemy, two volleys of javelins were thrown to disable as many as possible. Then, with swords drawn and ranks tightened behind an impenetrable wall of shields, the legion advanced to engage the enemy in close combat. The legionary's dagger served if his sword was lost, or to finish off a wounded enemy.

The javelin (*pilum*) was an ingenious weapon. Its long iron shank was designed to bend on impact so that it could not be thrown back by the enemy. The sharp point, if it did not kill or maim, could easily penetrate a shield and if the enemy could not quickly disengage the bent *pilum* from his shield, he would have to cast it aside and meet the Roman line without any defence.

The legionary wore his sword (*gladius*) high on the right side of his body. This enabled it to be drawn underarm with his right hand without interfering with the shield which he carried with his left. The sword was short (no more than 50cm), and its sturdy iron blade was double edged [4]. It was designed to be used with a stabbing action, but could also deal an effective slashing blow. The hand-grip was carved from wood or bone, and the heavy pommel could be of wood or even ivory. The scabbard - made of wood, bound in leather and with brass trim - was attached by four rings to a narrow shoulder-belt [1].

The legionary's broad, buckled waist-belt (*cingulum*) carried a dagger on the left side, and incorporated the apron of studded leather straps which gave some protection to the private parts [1,2]. The dagger (*pugio*) had a short, wide iron blade and a handle shaped from iron or brass sheet [2,3]; its scabbard was often highly decorated with enamel or silver inlay.

At barracks, the soldiers of each *contubernium* kept their personal equipment in the small storeroom which was paired with their sleeping-quarters. The cost of repairs and replacements were met by stoppages from pay - always the best encouragement for a soldier to take good care of his equipment.

ARTILLERY

To wear down the enemy at long range, and to destroy their defences before the advance, the legion used a range of portable artillery pieces. All relied on the same basic principle of storing energy in twisted skeins of horse-hair and animal sinew. The projectiles were either sturdy, iron-tipped arrows (bolts), or shot - round stones of up to a hundredweight. The larger the machine, the larger or longer the projectile it could fire; and the range of a single machine could be set simply by tightening or loosening the skeins. A legion may have had as many as seventy artillery pieces in its armoury - probably one light *catapulta* for every century, and one large machine (a *ballista* or, perhaps, an *onager*) for each cohort.

The basic light field artillery was the *catapulta* [2] which required a team of only two or three for its operation. It fired a small bolt (about 70cm long, with wooden flights and sharp 'armour-piercing' iron tip) over 500 metres with deadly accuracy, and could pick off individual targets. Its nickname, 'the scorpion' (*scorpio*), refered to the sharp 'sting' - the bolt - with which it killed.

Both the *catapulta* and its larger relation, the *ballista* [1], shared the same mechanism. The frame, of wood bound with iron, carried a strong front assembly with a pair of coils, vertically-set, to power the twin arms. The string was caught on a trigger mechanism and drawn back by a windlass and ratchet; the bolt or shot was placed in a groove and fired through an aperture in the front 'plate'. The whole frame pivotted on its support for rapid aim. Smaller *ballistae* could fire either bolts or shot for anti-personnel use in the field; larger pieces served in siege warfare.

The heavy *onager* [3], which was less manoeuvreable than the catapults but of more devastating effect, became more popular in a later period. Its one arm was powered by a single, horizontal skein and drawn back by windlass and ratchet; the boulder - or other unpleasant missile - was cradled in a sling suspended from the end of the arm. When the trigger was pulled, the arm shot forward onto a straw-filled cushion and, with massive recoil, sent the boulder flying in a high arc. The *onager* takes its nickname from the wild ass (*onager*), both from its 'kick', and from the ass's habit (so Roman writers tell us) of kicking up stones in the face of its pursuers.

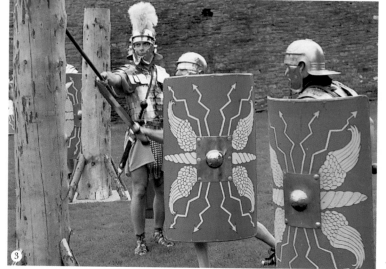

AT CAMP

The 25 years which a legionary devoted to the service of the emperor might all be spent on frontiers far from his family and home. The army provided for a soldier's welfare and morale - and encouraged bonds of comradeship and loyalty [1,4]. The daily routine was hard, with its constant round of weapons training [3] and a variety of tasks, both necessary and invented, to avoid the dangers of boredom and unrest.

In peacetime, all was done by rota and to a discipline enforced by the centurions. For the non-specialist, some duties were strictly military - as sentries at headquarters, as road patrols and escorts, or on detached service. But many were mundane chores connected with the efficient running of the camp: cleaning the latrines, stoking furnaces at the baths, or sweeping-out the barracks - and there was always kit to be polished for morning parade.

The soldiers' diet was ample and varied. At camp, wheat was the staple. This was ground into a coarse flour using rotary hand-mills [2], and the unleavened bread was baked in the century's ovens. The main cooked meal, taken in the evening, might include meat (beef, mutton, bacon or chicken), pulses, and a variety of fresh vegetables - and was washed down with wine or local beer.

The social life of the baths, and games at the amphitheatre, brought the pleasures of town life to camp. But every soldier longed for leave - to sleep, to visit friends and family, to tend to his financial affairs, or to squander his money on women, drink and gambling. A bribe to the centurion often assisted an application. Then, a soldier could find entertainment of all kinds in the civil settlement (*canabae*) outside the fortress - at brothels, taverns and the marketplace - or attend to personal worship at the temples of his many gods.

Legionaries were not allowed to marry - but many formed lasting relationships with local women and had children by them. These unofficial 'marriages' were tolerated by the authorities, who saw the male children as potential recruits to the legion, and could be made legal on the legionary's retirement. For such men, and for their sons - as recruits 'born at camp' - the fortress had really become their home.

15

TRAINING

Legionaries were fighting men, first and foremost. Constant and rigorous training kept them at peak condition, and ready for action at all times. Their regular physical exercise included running, jumping and swimming across rivers or in the sea - often in full kit and carrying a heavy pack.

Soldiers attended weapons drill every morning - and twice daily for new recruits. They trained at stout wooden posts, six feet high, which they were encouraged to treat as a real opponent [page 14.3]. Dummy swords and javelins made of wood, and wickerwork shields were of double the normal weight to improve their strength. Once recruits had learnt the proper use of these weapons they could move on to mock combat [1,2], eventually in full armour and with blunted service weapons. Soldiers were trained in basic horsemanship, the use of the bow and sling-shot, and even the art of throwing stones, for all could come in useful in battle.

On the parade ground, the legionary was taught to march in step and to obey instinctively the orders of his centurion. Here the recruit learned to act as one with his comrades-in-arms, in their many complicated formations.

Three times every month the legion assembled in full battle-dress for field manoeuvres which simulated campaign conditions [4]. For this the soldier became a 'beast of burden', carrying kit which might include wooden stakes, a saw, entrenching-tool and basket, chain, scythe and axe, as well as his personal rations and cooking equipment. With this load, he was required to march 20 Roman miles in five hours. At special training grounds, combined forces could conduct mock battles and sieges on a large scale.

Once trained, a soldier on campaign would have to raise the defences of a temporary camp wherever his army stopped, and however far he had marched. The *contubernium* then shared a goat-skin tent - the *papilio* or 'butterfly' [3] - which was carried by a mule with other communal equipment. Even for an overnight stop, the tents were laid out in the same strict order as at the fortress - for, as in everything the Roman army did, it was essential that the individual knew his place in the order of things.

FORMATIONS

To one contemporary commentator, legionary manoeuvres were simply 'bloodless battles' and real battle was no more than a 'manoeuvre' in which blood was spilled. Above all, soldiers practised the formations of the set-piece battle in open field at which the legions excelled. In formation, the men advanced as a body to break up, and then smash the enemy lines. Each soldier provided support for the men next to him - and all relied on the proper and coordinated use of the legionary's large shield.

The 'wedge' [1] is still used by riot police today to break up crowds. To the Romans, this aggressive formation was the 'pig's head', which enabled small groups of soldiers to 'snout' through the enemy line - pushing their opponents down with a wall of shields, and butchering them with their short swords. When expanded, the wedge allowed the mass of Roman forces to advance deep into enemy ranks - to split them in two, and to push them apart.

Things did not always go as planned, however, and it was important that defensive formations came automatically, too. If a body of men was surrounded by the enemy, they formed into the 'square'. Protected on all sides by interlocking shields, and with their javelins set like pikes at all angles, this 'prickly hedgehog' was especially effective against cavalry.

Perhaps the most remarkable formation was the aptly-named 'tortoise' (testudo). Its impenetrable shell was quickly formed by a body of men in close rank and file, with shields locked tightly together at front and over their heads, if not at their sides as well [3,4]. The testudo enabled legionaries to approach the very foot of enemy fortifications, protected from the inevitable rain of missiles hurled at them by the defenders.

In the line of battle, the legions occupied the centre ground, with auxiliaries at their flanks, cavalry posted to the 'wings', and reserves in the rear. In close order the line could extend to over a kilometre, and was several ranks deep. In open order, the lines were staggered, so that the men of the second line balanced the gaps of the front [2]. It was essential to the battle-line, as to all these formations, that every man was trained to fight with sword in his right hand and shield in his left - whatever his natural inclination.

OFFICERS

The Roman army had a clearly defined command structure, from the emperor down to the 'ordinary ranks'. It was the centurions - mostly elevated from the ranks - who provided the continuity of tradition essential to a disciplined fighting force. Often conservative and brutal, they were always feared - and frequently hated - by their men.

The first aim of the ambitious legionary was the privileged status of a 'specialist' (an *immunis*), with less rigorous duties and with up to twice the normal pay. Most progressed within the three grades of the century below that of centurion: *tesserarius* (guard commander), *signifer* (standard-bearer), and *optio* ('centurion in waiting'). The *optio* [3] was nominated by the centurion as his deputy. His knob-ended staff was used to prod the ranks into line; and he carried the 'orders of the day' in a pouch at his belt.

The centurion [1,2,4] was marked out by the transverse crest on his helmet, a shirt of mail or scale armour over a leather arming-doublet, and a cloak of fine material. His shin-guards and highly-decorated belt were silver-plated. The centurion wore his sword on the left and dagger on the right - in reverse fashion to the legionary - and the vine stick (*vitis*) which he carried, as a badge of rank, could be used viciously on the backs of idle soldiers. As today, officers were decorated for valour in battle [4]: a golden crown, perhaps, or a pair of silver *torques* (Celtic neck-rings), or a set of silvered medals (*phalerae*). The centurion's pay was at least fifteen times that of a legionary.

The most favoured centurions rose to command the first century of the First Cohort as *primus pilus*, the senior centurion of the legion, charged with the protection of its golden eagle-standard. A final promotion to 'camp prefect' (*praefectus castrorum*) could follow - as second in command to the legate himself.

The legate and his six staff officers (tribunes) were men of the ruling classes - senators and equestrians ('knights') - whose short-term commissions offered experience for the highest positions in military and civil life which it was their duty to fill. At the fortress, the legate and his tribunes lived in comfortable, large houses - and in a social class apart from the soldiers and centurions.

STANDARD-BEARERS

The standards embodied the very 'souls' of their units, and were revered by the men and fiercely protected. A golden eagle (*aquila*) was the symbol of the legion as a whole, and each of the 59 centuries had its own spear-standard (*signum*). A standard bearing an image of the emperor (the *imago*) served to identify him to his troops, and to focus their loyalty on him, as dictator [3].

In battle, the tall centurial standards served as rallying points for the men. Loud blasts on the horn (*cornu*) would draw eyes to the standard which, with movements, could be used to convey simple commands [2]. The standards were drawn up together to lead the army on the march. In peacetime, all of the legion's standards were held together in the 'chapel of the standards' at the headquarters, firmly clasped to its walls.

To carry any of the sacred standards was a mark of special honour. Standard-bearers and musicians (like the horn-blower, or *cornicen*) normally wore shirts of mail or scale armour. As mark of their status, and to convey appropriate ferocity, they wore the skins of bears or wolves. Standard-bearers had a specific responsibility for the safekeeping of soldiers' pay and savings - and for that, too, they had to enjoy the trust of the men. The eagle-carrier (*aquilifer*) was responsible for the legionary pay-chest which was held, for security from violation, close to the chapel of the standards. The eagle-symbol never left the camp unless the whole legion moved out on campaign or to a new base - for where it went, there the legion was.

The centurial standard-bearer (*signifer*) was also a man of exemplary character and good education. As officer responsible for the men's savings, his paperwork included issuing receipts for deposits and preparing detailed accounts. For armour, he may have worn a shirt of small brass scales sewn to a linen undergarment, and certainly a bearskin [1].

The centurial standard (*signum*) took the form of a spear-shaft decorated with a number of silvered medallions including, perhaps, the 'badge' of the legion. It was often topped by the sign of a hand, palm-forward, as a reminder to the soldiers of the gesture of loyalty which they made at their oath-taking.

AUXILIARIES

The Romans were quick to employ the fighting skills of the peoples that they conquered - Thracian horsemen, Syrian archers, and slingers from the Balearic Islands. Such auxiliary troops became part of the established structure of the army, but continued to draw recruits from the non-citizen population - and mainly from the barbarian inhabitants of the frontier areas of the empire.

The annual pay of an auxiliary soldier was probably only one-third that of the legionary and he received no cash grant on his retirement. So why did men choose to enlist? The service regime of the *auxilia* was certainly less arduous than in the legions. But what attracted above all was the grant of Roman citizenship given to every auxiliary on his retirement. This citizenship passed to his children and heirs forever, and was a reward of elevated status that no money could buy. For that end, a recruit may have spent his 25 years' service far from his homeland - a distrustful administration preferred to see these non-Roman soldiers placed far from any local loyalties.

There were three types of auxiliary unit - light infantry (a *cohors* or cohort), part-mounted infantry (a *cohors equitata*), and front-line cavalry (an *ala*). Each regiment was commanded by a prefect (*praefectus*) or tribune, who answered to the legionary commanders. Infantry cohorts were formed on the legionary model, with either six or ten centuries (i.e. of strength 480 and 800) each led by a centurion [3].

The auxiliary infantryman was distinguished by a uniform that reflected his unit's origin and specialist function [1]. Most wore a simple mail or scale shirt over their tunic, perhaps with trousers of leather or wool. His helmet, sword and dagger were similar to those of the legionary but perhaps less highly-ornamented. For lightness and agility, he carried a flat oval shield - often brightly decorated - and was equipped with a stabbing-spear (*hasta*).

The *auxilia* provided the legions with an essential complement of light and fast-moving troops - and all of the fighting cavalry. They could support the legions in the battle-line - where sometimes they were no more than 'cannon-fodder' - or function independently of them on frontier and other policing duties [2].

CAVALRY

The power and speed of the horse have always placed the cavalryman among an army's élite. The Romans relied for their cavalry on auxiliary troops drawn from nations with a tradition of horsemanship - from Thrace and Scythia to North Africa. These were standardised into the auxiliary unit called an *ala* - the Latin word for 'wing'.

The *alae* were a strike-force whose normal position in battle was at the flanks (or 'wings') of the legion. Placed there, the fast-moving cavalry could encircle the enemy, to force them into direct confrontation with the front-line, or prevent the enemy from out-flanking the Roman forces. The cavalry really came into its own when pursuing a retreating enemy in disarray.

The essential unit of the *ala* was a troop (*turma*), probably of 32 men, led by a decurion and each with its own standard-bearer. An *ala* of normal strength comprised 16 troops (or 512 horse) and was commanded by a high-ranking prefect. A very few units - the prestigious *ala milliaria* - comprised one thousand horse (24 *turmae*).

Roman horses were scarcely more than ponies but were carefully selected for breed, size, fitness and age. The Romans did not have use of the stirrup, and the leather saddle was provided instead with four tall 'horns' to give the rider a good seat. The horse's leather harness was richly decorated with silvered pendants and medallions [1,3].

Typically a cavalryman wore a shirt of mail or scale armour over a jerkin, with tight-fitting trousers and a knotted neck-scarf. His flat, oval shield [3] could be suspended from the saddle, and his weapons were two stabbing-spears (*hastae*), perhaps a quiver of throwing-darts, and a long, slashing-sword (*spatha*). His helmet of iron or bronze could be extravagantly decorated - sometimes with human features [2].

Together horse and man trained to jump ditches and walls, to swim, and perform their manoeuvres with precision - and to remain calm in the confusion of battle. Colourful 'sports-days' - rather like medieval tournaments - celebrated 'pay-days' and religious festivals. For these, both horse and rider wore elaborate face-masks, and performed feats which tested their skills to the full.

BATTLE

In A.D.60, there was rebellion in Britain. Boudica, the queen of the Iceni, led several tribes of southern England who were united in their revulsion at corrupt Roman rule. Unrestrained, they destroyed the new Roman settlements at Colchester, St.Albans and London. The provincial governor, Suetonius Paulinus - who was campaigning in North Wales - rushed back to quell the revolt with an army of some 10,000 men. The Roman historian Tacitus describes the battle:

'Suetonius decided to attack without delay. He chose a position in a valley with a wood behind him. There could be no enemy, he knew, except at his front, where there was open country without cover for ambushes. Suetonius drew up the legionaries in close order, with the auxiliaries at their flanks, and the cavalry massed on the wings. On the British side, cavalry and infantry bands seethed over a wide area in unprecedented numbers [1,2]. Their confidence was such that they brought their wives with them to see the victory, installing them in carts stationed at the edge of the battlefield.

Suetonius appealed to his men. "Disregard the clamours and empty threats of the natives! ... Just keep in close order. Throw your javelins, and then carry on: use shield-bosses to fell them, swords to kill them. Do not think of plunder. When you have won, you will have everything."

He gave the order for battle. At first the legionaries stood their ground. Keeping to the valley as a natural defence, they launched their javelins accurately at the approaching enemy. Then, in wedge formation, they burst forward [3]. So did the auxiliary infantry. The cavalry, with lances extended, demolished all serious resistance [4]. The remaining Britons fled with difficulty since their ring of wagons blocked their escape. The Romans did not spare even the women. Baggage animals too, transfixed with weapons, added to the heaps of dead. It was a glorious victory.'

The Romans' superiority of discipline and tactics assured them victory over the chaotic mass of the Britons. Suetonius chose the field of battle to his advantage, and employed his specialist forces - the legions, *auxilia* and cavalry - in set-piece manoeuvres, and without mercy.

PEACE UNDER ROME

Rome intended Britain to become a productive and peaceful part of its empire. Conquest by treaty and by warfare was only a beginning - conquered barbarians had now to adopt Roman ways.

Soldiers introduced Roman tastes and habits, particularly in the civilian settlements which grew around the forts and fortresses. Sometimes these settlements thrived even after the army had moved on, to grow into market towns, At new city-colonies of retired legionaries the Britons found a model of Roman urban life which they were encouraged to emulate. Tacitus describes the provincial governor's schemes of social and economic improvement:

'Agricola's object was to accustom the people to a life of peace and quiet by the provision of amenities. He gave private encouragement and official assistance to the building of temples, public squares, and good houses.... He educated the sons of the chiefs in the liberal arts.... The result was that instead of loathing the Latin language they became eager to speak it effectively. In the same way, our national dress came into favour and the toga was everywhere to be seen. And so the population was gradually led into the demoralizing temptations of arcades, baths and sumptuous banquets. The unsuspecting Britons spoke of such novelties as 'civilization', when in fact they were only a feature of their enslavement.'

The Britons were ultimately trusted to administer their own affairs on a local level. Magistrates and councillors, elected from the property-owning class, raised fine public buildings in the towns which now served as their tribal capitals. All answered to Rome via the governor - whose toga bore the broad purple stripe which distinguished him as a senator [4]. The wealthy few enjoyed a fully Roman lifestyle - with a fine house in town, and perhaps a luxurious country villa as centre of their agricultural estate. Women, as well as men, adopted provincial Roman dress [1,3].

But the great majority of the population were peasants for whom the coming of Rome brought peace and the imposition of taxes, but little else. They retained their language, their habits and customs, and continued to worship their old gods. For these, some of whom continued to live in their traditional round houses [2], 'Romanisation' was a thin veneer indeed.

CAERLEON - ROMAN ISCA

With the establishment of frontier zones with a potentially unruly population, came the need for a standing garrison with permanent accommodation. Forts (of 1-5ha) were built for each auxiliary unit, and a fortress (of some 20ha) for each of the legions. All shared the same rectilinear arrangement of streets and buildings which originated in the layout of tents at the temporary camps.

For over two hundred years, *legio II Augusta* had its base at Caerleon [1], near Newport in South Wales - giving it the Celtic name *Isca*, from the River Usk on which it stood. The fortress was founded in A.D.74 or 75, soon after the final conquest of the Silures by the governor Julius Frontinus. *Isca* was intended to provide fitting and permanent accommodation for one of the four legions then assigned to control Britain.

For speed of construction, many buildings at *Isca* were first built of timber. But it was always intended that these should be replaced by durable stone buildings when manpower allowed. Great works of architecture were involved - particularly at the baths and headquarters - and, with other calls on manpower, the task was to take almost twenty-five years.

The fortress contained all of the buildings necessary for the accommodation, administration, provision and welfare of the legion - barracks [3] for each of the 59 centuries, a palace for the legate, houses for the officers, factories, granaries, large baths and even a hospital. All was defended by a ditch and a walled rampart, with regularly spaced watch-towers and imposing gateways. Beyond the defences lay the amphitheatre and parade-ground, the civil settlements and cemeteries.

Today, the small town of Caerleon ('City of the Legion') covers only part of the fortress, which is quite shallowly buried. Archaeological excavations since the 1920s have uncovered much of the Roman plan, and have exposed important remains to public view - the amphitheatre, part of the fortress wall, several barracks and the imposing fortress baths. Modern excavations [2; at the fortress baths, 1979] continue to tell us more about the architecture and history of *Isca* and of the daily life of the soldiers of *legio II Augusta* for whom this place was once home.

EVIDENCE

How do we know what Roman soldiers looked like - or how they lived their lives? We can only build up a *picture* of the past from contemporary writings, from inscriptions and sculpture, and from the evidence of archaeology. This evidence doesn't always fit together very neatly - and, whatever new discoveries are made, will never provide the answers to all the questions we would like to ask.

Roman historians were often more interested in literary style than in the mere technical details of warfare. Even the well-informed Tacitus rarely discussed detail of the army, for that was already well known to his readers. A military manual written by Vegetius tells us of the structure of the first-century legions - but he lived three hundred years later, and misunderstood the old records which he used. Occasionally, military documents are preserved on papyrus or wooden tablets - accounts of soldiers' pay and savings, postings, duty-rosters, and even personal letters.

For our image of the Roman army in action, the prime source is Trajan's Column, erected in Rome in A.D.113[4]. Its sculpted frieze illustrates the progress of Trajan's successful campaigns against the Dacians (in modern-day Romania), and records the army at all its activities - in battle, building camps, foraging for food, felling trees, and on the march.

Sculpted gravestones give us individual histories and show what equipment was appropriate to a particular rank. The gravestone of M. Favonius Facilis [1], centurion of legion *XX*, provides the basis for the modern reconstruction on page 25. Rufus Sita [3] was a trooper of the Sixth Cohort of Thracians, a part-mounted unit - his gravestone shows him riding down a naked Celtic warrior, and tells us that he died *'aged 40 years, after 22 years service'*.

Archaeology - the study of the material remains of the past - tells us something of the soldiers' experience. The planning of Roman forts and fortresses reflects the organisation of army units, and their official activities; the evidence of animal bones and plant remains tells us of their diet. An inscription on a bronze cooking-pan from Caerleon [2] shows that it belonged to a trooper of the First *Ala* of Thracians; and finds of military equipment fill in the details of a soldier's kit - lost fittings from his armour, or fragments of his weapons.

THE ERMINE STREET GUARD

The men and women who appear in this book are modern people who aim to recreate only the physical appearance of the Roman army - but not to live like Romans. *The Ermine Street Guard* is an amateur society committed to researching and reproducing the equipment and drill of the Roman imperial army of the late first century A.D. Their rigorous standards of authenticity give us, in the late twentieth century, our most vivid image of how the Roman army may have looked.

The origins of the society go back to 1972, when the Gloucestershire parishes of Witcombe and Bentham organised a costume pageant to raise funds for a new village hall. Eight men proudly paraded as Roman soldiers. Their interest sparked, the men soon made contact with H. Russell Robinson, author of the authoritative work on Roman armour. Recognising their enthusiasm and potential, he shared the results of his experimental reconstructions. Encouraged to abandon mere costumes in favour of accurate replicas, *The Ermine Street Guard* was on its way. Today, the Guard is a registered charity, able to turn out forty men (and women) in full uniform for educational displays and media appearances.

The armour and equipment of *The Ermine Street Guard* is almost exclusively made by its members, using modern tools, but with materials kept as near to the original as possible. The results are a valuable form of experimental archaeology. They demonstrate, for instance, both the great practicality and flexibility of the plate armour, and its need for constant maintenance.

The construction of communal equipment, such as the artillery pieces and tent, can answer other practical questions - 'What was the range of a *catapulta*?'; 'Was a leather tent really waterproof?'; 'How much did it weigh?'. In 1993, in consultation with archaeological experts, the Guard made the first ever accurate, hand-stitched reconstruction of an 8-man, goat-skin tent - it is waterproof; it required 77 complete goat-hides, and it weighs 40kg.

Every year the exciting spectacle of *The Ermine Street Guard* brings the Roman army alive for thousands of visitors to historic sites and museums both in this country and abroad. They have won the respect and admiration of the public and academic world alike.